THE HISTORY OF THE NEW YORK GIANTS

THE HISTORY OF THE
NEW YORK

Published by Creative Education

123 South Broad Street

Mankato, Minnesota 56001

Creative Education is an imprint of The Creative Company.

DESIGN AND PRODUCTION BY **EVANSDAY DESIGN**

LIBRARY OF CONGRESS CATALOGING-IN-PUBLICATION DATA

Goodman, Michael E.

The history of the New York Giants / by Michael E. Goodman.

p. cm. — (NFL today)

Summary: Traces the history of the team from its beginnings through 2003.

ISBN 1-58341-306-5

1. New York Giants (Football team)—History—Juvenile literature. [1. New York

Giants (Football team)—History. 2. Football—History.] I. Title. II. Series.

GV956.N368G66 2004

796.332'64'097471—dc22   2003065037

First edition

9 8 7 6 5 4 3 2 1

COVER PHOTO: defensive end Michael Strahan

GIANTS

THERE IS NO BETTER WORD TO DESCRIBE NEW YORK CITY THAN GIANT. WITH A POPULATION OF AROUND EIGHT MILLION PEOPLE, NEW YORK IS THE LARGEST CITY IN THE UNITED STATES AND THE HOME OF SOME OF ITS LARGEST BUSINESSES, MOST IMPRESSIVE THEATERS AND SHOPS, AND MOST EXPENSIVE RESTAURANTS. NOWHERE IN THE COUNTRY WILL A PERSON FIND LARGER CROWDS, BIGGER TRAFFIC JAMS, OR NOISIER SPORTS FANS.

SINCE 1925, MANY OF THE LOUDEST FANS HAVE BEEN THOSE CHEERING FOR THE NEW YORK GIANTS OF THE NATIONAL FOOTBALL LEAGUE (NFL). THE TEAM PLAYED ITS FIRST GAMES IN THE POLO GROUNDS, THE PLACE MAJOR LEAGUE BASEBALL'S NEW YORK GIANTS CALLED HOME. SO THE TEAM'S FIRST OWNER CALLED HIS CLUB THE GIANTS, TOO. THE BASEBALL GIANTS MOVED TO SAN FRANCISCO LONG AGO, BUT THE FOOTBALL TEAM THAT FANS AFFECTIONATELY CALL "THE JINTS" HAS BEEN CREATING BIG-TIME EXCITEMENT IN NEW YORK FOR MORE THAN 75 YEARS.

[Safety Emlen Tunnell]

IN 1925, a New York businessman and sports promoter named Tim Mara tried to buy a part-interest in a top professional boxer named Gene Tunney. When his bid was turned down, Mara was convinced to buy a franchise in the new NFL instead. At the time, football was mainly a college sport, and no one knew if a pro team would attract fans and make money in New York. But the $500 price tag for the club seemed like a bargain to Mara. "I figured that even an empty store in New York City was worth more than $500," he said.

During the Giants' first season at the Polo Grounds, Mara had to give away almost as many tickets as he sold just so the stands wouldn't be empty. The Giants started out 0–3 and then hit their stride. Behind running backs Jack McBride and Henry Haines, the club finished the 1925 season with an 8–4 record.

Before coaching the Giants for 23 years, Steve Owen (right) was team captain as a player in the 1920s^

The Giants continued to improve on the field but to do poorly at the ticket office. Yet Mara agreed to stick with his "bargain." He was thrilled when his club earned its first NFL title in 1927 by posting a league-best 11–1–1 record. That championship team was coached by Earl Potteiger and featured Hall-of-Famer Morris "Red" Badgro at offensive and defensive end.

In 1931, Mara appointed defensive tackle Steve Owen as player-coach and gave him a long-term contract. Owen would remain the Giants' head coach for the next 23 years. The club also outbid two other teams for the services of two-way star Mel Hein by offering him $150 a game. Hein went on to play every minute of every Giants game for the next 15 years, serving as both center and linebacker. "And in all that time, I can count on the fingers of one hand the mistakes he made offensively and defensively," said Coach Owen.

Owen's teams, anchored by Hein and quarterback Ed Danowski, won eight NFL Eastern Division titles between 1933 and 1946 and captured the league championship in 1934 and 1938. Tim Mara's bargain had turned out to be a bonanza.

THE GLORY YEARS>

FOLLOWING OWEN'S RETIREMENT in 1953, former Giants end Jim Lee Howell took over as head coach and began rebuilding the Giants. Howell inherited a solid nucleus with quarterback Charlie Conerly, running back Frank Gifford, and offensive tackle Roosevelt Brown. He then engineered trades for fullback Alex Webster, defensive end Andy Robustelli, and linebacker Sam Huff. These players were the core of the Giants team that celebrated its move to Yankee Stadium in 1956 by winning the NFL championship.

Boot ◁10◁ Boot 10! Set! Hut Hut!

Versatile fullback Alex Webster (with ball) spent 10 seasons with the Giants in the 1950s and '60s^

Gifford, who starred in that championship game victory over the Chicago Bears, was named the NFL's Player of the Year in 1956. The talented Californian with movie-star looks was the team's top scorer, runner, and pass receiver that season. He even tossed two touchdown passes. "Frank was the body and soul of our team," said Coach Howell. "He was the player we went to in the clutch."

Two years later, Gifford led the Giants back to another NFL title game. This time, New York faced off against the Baltimore Colts in a contest that has been called "The Greatest Game Ever Played." The two clubs featured a combined 15 future members of the Pro Football Hall of Fame. Fittingly, the game went into sudden-death overtime, with the Colts eking out a 23–17 win. More important was the fact that millions of people watched the dramatic game on television that day, and many of them became new fans of pro football. "We didn't know it at the time," said NFL commissioner Pete Roselle, "but it was the beginning for the NFL. From that game forward, our fan base grew and grew. We owe both franchises a huge debt."

Team owner Tim Mara died a few weeks after the championship loss, but his sons Jack and Wellington continued to direct the club. The Mara sons oversaw a changing of the guard at Yankee Stadium. First, Coach Howell decided to retire after the 1960 season and was replaced by assistant coach Allie Sherman. Sherman then traded with the San Francisco 49ers for 35-year-old quarterback Y. A. Tittle.

The 49ers thought Tittle was past his prime, but he found new life in New York. In 1961, the "old man" led the Giants to a 10–3–1 record and was named the NFL's Most Valuable Player. Tittle led New York to three straight Eastern Division titles between 1961 and 1963, although the club came up short in the NFL championship game each time.

In 1963, quarterback Y.A. Tittle tossed 36 touchdown passes, setting a franchise record that still stands^

OVER THE NEXT 15 years, the Giants went through four coaches and five quarterbacks and put together just two winning seasons. New York fans began to wonder if the club would ever escape the National Football Conference (NFC) Eastern Division cellar. Even a move in 1976 to Giants Stadium, a new 76,000-seat stadium in nearby New Jersey, could not change the team's luck.

The Giants featured several outstanding offensive players during those down years, including scrambling quarterback Fran Tarkenton, tight end Bob Tucker, and running back Ron Johnson. Yet the club's defense was in shambles. The offense could not put up enough points to offset the amount the defense gave up.

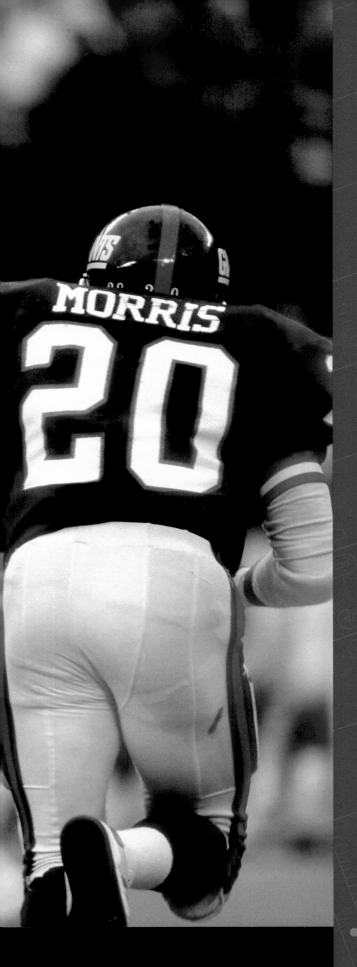

The Giants' prospects finally began looking up when George Young came on board in 1979 as the team's general manager. Young had a reputation for building successful NFL teams. But Giants fans questioned his first big move: selecting Phil Simms, an unknown quarterback from Morehead State College in Kentucky, as the team's top pick in the 1979 NFL Draft. The next day, newspaper headlines throughout the New York area read: "Phil Who?"

During the next 14 seasons, New Yorkers would come to appreciate Simms for his talent, courage, and unique ability to perform in the clutch. Before the star quarterback retired, he would carve his name into the Giants record book in nearly every passing category.

SIMMS'S ARRIVAL IN New York signaled the start of a rise back to respectability. But it was Young's top draft choice in 1981—linebacker Lawrence Taylor—that really helped turn the Giants into one of the NFL's most exciting and feared teams.

As a child in Williamsburg, Virginia, Lawrence Taylor had signed up for a local Jaycees football team. After the coach assigned him to play linebacker, "L.T." went to the library to read stories about famous pro linebackers and learn about the position. "I read how they saw the game, what their feeling was, and what their tempo was," Taylor recalled. "I got the concept right then that, aside from being smart, a good linebacker was also mean."

One of the most intimidating players of all time, Lawrence Taylor was an almost unstoppable force.

Receiver and punt returner Phil McConkey helped make 1986 a Giants season to remember^

ıııııı Dive ⟨22⟩ Dive 22! Set! Hut Hut! ıııııııııııııııı

Mark Bavaro was famous for his brute strength ^

Bill Parcells won 85 games as Giants head coach ^

During the 13 years that L.T. starred for the Giants, no NFL linebacker was smarter, meaner, or tougher than Taylor. Opposing teams hoping to keep their quarterback healthy always had to make stopping Taylor their first priority. "What he really did was change the way other teams looked at our defense," said Bill Parcells, who became the Giants' head coach in 1983. "He scared them is what he did."

With Simms powering the offense and Taylor heading the defense, the Giants made the play-offs in 1984 and 1985. In 1986, Phil McConkey emerged as one of the league's most dangerous receivers, and Taylor was named the NFL's Most Valuable Player after making 20.5 quarterback sacks. Also starring that season were running back Joe Morris, who rushed for a club-record 1,516 yards, and tight end Mark Bavaro, who rumbled for more than 1,000 yards on pass receptions and delivered devastating blocks. These players carried New York to a 14–2 record.

The Giants crushed the San Francisco 49ers and Washington Redskins in the playoffs to earn the right to meet the Denver Broncos in the Super Bowl. In the Super Bowl, Simms played the finest game of his life. He completed a remarkable 22 of 25 passes (a record 88 percent) to lead New York to a 39–20 victory and its first NFL title in 30 years.

Coach Parcells's crew had one more terrific run in 1990. By then, the coach had begun shifting the Giants' offensive philosophy toward a low-risk rushing attack. "I knew the game was changing," Parcells said. "There are too many multiple defenses these days. You're better off just lining up with your big guys and pounding away."

With running backs Joe Morris and Ottis Anderson taking handoffs from Simms and following their massive blockers, the Giants ground down their opponents. The strategy worked well enough to return the Giants to the Super Bowl. In the championship game against the Buffalo Bills, New York eked out a hard-fought 20–19 victory for the Giants' sixth NFL championship.

The club went into a decline in the early 1990s as, one by one, the team's former stars suffered injuries or moved on. When both Simms and Taylor hung up their Giants jerseys at the end of the 1993 season, another golden era had ended.

Ottis Anderson earned Super Bowl Most Valuable Player honors in 1990 by grinding out 102 rushing yards.

IN 1997, a year after New York went just 6–10, the Giants hired offensive specialist Jim Fassel as their new head coach. Fassel's first squad got off to a 1–3 start, and fans in Giants Stadium booed loudly. But Fassel refused to make drastic changes. "The little red panic button is always there if you want to reach up and push it," he said. "But I would have lost them right then if I started to make wholesale changes.... Everything I had told them about being consistent and staying the course would have gone out the window."

The boos quickly turned to cheers as Fassel's new offensive system began to click. Led by quarterback Danny Kanell, the team finished the 1997 season 10–5–1. In just one year, Coach Fassel had helped lift the team from last place to first place in the NFC East.

A big passer known for his powerful arm, Kerry Collins took over as quarterback in the late '90s^

Tiki Barber gained a team-record 2,089 yards in 2000 by rushing, receiving, and returning kicks ^

Ike Hilliard boosted the 2002 Giants with his speed ^

Michael Strahan made an NFL-record 22.5 sacks in 2001 ^

Once they had learned how to win, Fassel's Giants refused to slide back down the standings. By 2000, the team was ready for another championship run. Led by quarterback Kerry Collins and running back Tiki Barber on offense and end Michael Strahan on defense, the 2000 Giants went 12–4 to win another division title. In the playoffs, the "Jints" swept by the Philadelphia Eagles and Minnesota Vikings to reach the Super Bowl, where they faced the Baltimore Ravens. New York's exciting run stopped there, however, as the fierce Ravens defense shut down the Giants in a 34–7 rout.

In the 2002 NFL Draft, the Giants found another offensive standout: 6-foot-5 and 255-pound tight end Jeremy Shockey. The rookie was an instant star, leading all NFL tight ends in receptions (74) and receiving yards (894). Known for his fiery personality, he was also the league's "trash-talking" leader. Shockey's ability to catch passes and carry defenders on his back for big gains helped open up the field for other Giants receivers such as speedsters Ike Hilliard and Amani Toomer. The result was a 10–6 record and another trip to the playoffs.

In 2003, New York bolstered its defense by bringing in young lineman William Joseph. With Joseph added to an already talented lineup, the Giants had their sights set on big things in 2004 and beyond. "You'd be hard-pressed to find a better group," said

Collins. "I look around, there's Ike, there's Shock, there's Amani. I look behind me and there's Tiki…. I'll put this skilled group up against anybody."

The Giants, a team that entered the NFL as a $500 bargain more than 75 years ago, is today considered a priceless possession by millions of football fans throughout the New York metropolitan area. Backed by decades of rich history and the undying support of the vocal New York faithful, today's Giants—under the leadership of new head coach Tom Coughlin—plan to continue making big news in America's biggest city for years to come.

INDEX >

A

Anderson, Ottis 24, 24–25

B

Badgro, Morris (Red) 8
Barber, Tiki 28, 29, 31
Bavaro, Mark 23, 23
Brown, Roosevelt 10

C

Collins, Kerry 27, 29, 31
Conerly, Charlie 10, 12–13
Coughlin, Tom 31

D

Danowski, Ed 8
division championships 8, 14, 26, 29

F

Fassel, Jim 26, 29

G

Giants Stadium 16, 26
Gifford, Frank 10, 13

H

Haines, Henry 6
Hall of Fame 8, 13
Hein, Mel 8
Hilliard, Ike 29, 29, 31
Howell, Jim Lee 10, 13, 14
Huff, Sam 10

J

Johnson, Ron 16
Joseph, William 29

K

Kanell, Danny 26

M

Mara, Tim 6, 8, 14
McBride, Jack 6
McConkey, Phil 22, 23
Morris, Joe 23, 24

N

NFL championship games 13, 14
NFL championships 8, 10, 23, 24
NFL records 23

O

Owen, Steve 7, 8, 10

P

Parcells, Bill 23, 23, 24
Polo Grounds 4, 6
Potteiger, Earl 8

R

Robustelli, Andy 10
Roselle, Pete 13

S

Sherman, Allie 14
Shockey, Jeremy 8–9, 29, 31
Simms, Phil 18–19, 19, 20, 23, 24
Strahan, Michael 29, 29
Super Bowl 23, 24, 29

T

Tarkenton, Fran 16, 17
Taylor, Lawrence 20, 21, 23, 24
team records 19, 23
Tittle, Y.A. 14, 14–15
Toomer, Amani 29, 30–31, 31
Tucker, Bob 16
Tunnell, Emlen 5

W

Webster, Alex 10, 11

Y

Yankee Stadium 10, 14
Young, George 19, 20